Platfo

Gospel Sketches fo

Edited by Clifford Sharp

Nimbus Press

COPYRIGHT

We are mainly interested in providing resources for churches that want to use drama in worship, in bible study and in evangelism, and for Amateur Dramatic Groups. **You are free to perform any of our plays and sketches and do not need permission but we would appreciate receiving news of any productions. All our plays are protected by copyright and so we ask that you buy copies for each actor when you purchase one.** We hope that you will find them useful for the work of the Kingdom.

Fees for performances by professional companies will be subject to negotiation.

Published by Nimbus Press,
18 Guilford Road, Leicester, LE2 2RB
Cover illustration by Philip Spence

Copyright © Bennett et al 2000

British Library Cataloguing in Publication
Data available

ISBN 1 874424 47 0

Printed in Great Britain by
Saville Press Printers, Illiffe House, Illiffe Avenue,
Oadby, Leicester, LE2 5LS

Contents

Introduction

The first seven of these nine sketches are those that were highest placed (out of over eighty entries) in a competition organised by the Association of Christian Writers. The other two were commissioned from two of our regular authors. The sketches have all been written for performance in these early years of our new millennium when we are especially aware of time and its passing. The authors come from such different places as London and Hereford, Liverpool and Cambridgeshire. They include teachers, a former bus driver, a social worker, a student, an occupational therapist and an economist.

'The Good Traveller' is a witty 'head to head' modern version of the 'Good Samaritan' with a surprising twist at the end. 'It's about time' features a pot that does not want to be moulded by the master potter. 'The decision is yours' uses programmes similar to 'Do you want to be a millionaire?' and 'Mastermind' to present a challenge. 'The train now standing' is an amusing parable which asks us whether we want God to go on our holidays with us. 'Gods r us' pictures virtual reality religion that gets out of control. 'The Ladder' (which was the overall winner of the A.C.W. competition) contains a challenge to sort out the things in life that are passing away from those that are eternal. A businessman, a housewife and a woman minister all fail the test of how they would use their 'ladder'. 'Platform souls' is another rail-based parable about train spotters and what we will make of our future. 'Sale of the century' tells us what happens when a 'traveller' meets an accountant at lunchtime in the park. In 'A Place for the dinosaurs' two angels struggle with the new idea of time and with their part in planning God's new 'universe'. They are shocked to discover that some clever men will think that all their best designs just 'bubbled out of nothing'.

The Good Traveller

Sophie Bishop and Gary Kennedy

Characters

Jim

Pete

Bible background

Parable of the Good Samaritan.
'Teacher,' he asked, 'what must I do to receive eternal life?'
Luke 10.25-37

The scene is set over a table. Pete and Jim face each other.

Jim	Who was that at the door then?
Pete	What? Just then?
Jim	Yeah. The one you were shouting at.
Pete	Oh, just some woman who was bible-bashing.
Jim	Oh, right. So, what did she say then?
Pete	She said that I wasn't a Christian. What a nerve: just because I don't go to Church regularly. I nearly punched her on the nose!
Jim	So what stopped you then?
Pete	Well, she was bigger than me.
Jim	Anyway, I didn't know you went to Church at all.
Pete	I don't! But you don't have to go to Church to believe in God, do you?
Jim	I suppose not. *(Pause.)* I didn't know you believed in God.
Pete	Oh, yes. I'm always saying 'Thank God' for something or other.

Jim	That's right. And I often here you say 'Jesus Christ'.
Pete	Yeah, well! And you don't have to go to Church to pray. I mean you can pray anywhere, can't you? You could pray here, couldn't you? Or down the local. Or while you're walking. Or in Tesco. Or while you're standing at the bus stop. Or watching United. Or sitting on the loo.
Jim	Well, unless you have your mind on other things. *(Pause.)* So do you pray then?
Pete	No, of course not! What do you think I am then, some kind of fanatic?
Jim	So, what makes you a Christian then?
Pete	I got Christened when I was a baby. Always put myself down as C. of E.
Jim	But it takes more than that to make you a Christian, doesn't it?
Pete	What? What do you mean?
Jim	Well, I mean you've got to show it in some way, haven't you? I mean in the way you look after others.
Pete	Yes, oh yes. Absolutely. *(Pause.)* Er, so what do you mean?
Jim	Well, Jesus told this story about a geezer in his new Mercedes, who was travelling down to London for a business convention. He decides to keep off the motorways and takes a country road. Anyway, nature takes its course and he needs a Jimmy. So he stops his car and jumps out. When he gets back in there are these two other guys armed with knives and they take all he's got.
Pete	What? All his money?
Jim	All his money, his credit cards, the photographs of the children, his American Express. Everything.

Pete	So how do these two heavies get away?
Jim	They drive his Merc. But before they do they beat this posh geezer up, take all his clothes, and leave him for dead.
Pete	In the middle of the road.
Jim	Exactly. As luck would have it, a well-heeled Christian comes driving by in his new Land Rover. He sees the posh bloke lying there and slows down.
Pete	Oh, I know! He stops his car and takes him to hospital.
Jim	Not exactly. He slows down making sure he avoids running over the bloke. But he thinks the bloke's drunk. And anyway he's on his way to Church, and if he's not careful he'll be late.
Pete	You don't want to be late for a service now, do you? What would everybody think?
Jim	Not long after, a Baptist minister arrives at the scene. He jumps out of his car ...
Pete	... And rescues the poor, beaten up businessman.
Jim	No! He picks him up and moves him to the side of the road. Very carefully, mind you. He is on his way to a speaking engagement about helping those in need in the developing world.
Pete	Very noble! Somebody has to do it.
Jim	A third person can now be heard coming down the road.
Pete	Yes, yes. It's somebody from the good old Church of England.
Jim	Not quite. It's a New Age traveller. She's on her way to a psychic convention. She stops her rusting heap of metal and carefully lifts the bleeding body into the back of the junk pile. Crashing the gears she eventually reaches

7

	a local motel. She calls a doctor and even offers to pay for the bloke to stay there.
Pete	Didn't know he'd come out of a Merc.
Jim	Proper mess he was. So which of these three do you think was following Jesus?
Pete	It's obvious isn't it? The first two. They were off doing holy things, while the scruff in the rust heap was just some screwball, with totally heathen beliefs, scrounging off the social.
Jim	Sometimes, you know, I really don't know why I try.

END

It's About Time ...

Cara Grant

Characters

Pot *(Lump of clay with facial features and attitude.)*
Potter's Assistant *(An inexperienced helper at the pottery.*
Wears overall with 'PA' on front.)
Potter *(Wears overall with 'P' on.)*

Bible background

Spiritual treasure in clay pots.
'Does the clay ask the potter what he is doing?'
Isaiah 45.9-12   2 Corinthians 4.5-7

A pottery workshop. Potter's Assistant has a clipboard and pen, spectacles. Workbench labelled 'number 16'. This could be depicted by a box with a hole in the middle, through which Pot's head fits - the rest of him being concealed below. Pot wears grey / white face and hair colour.

> *Potter's Assistant bustles in, sifting through the pages of notes on his clipboard. Rushes past the workbench, then scurries back. Raises his specs to examine the workbench number and checks with his notes again.*

P.A.   Aha! Umm h'm, this is it - number sixteen - yes, just one or two odd bits to add on here for the Potter.

> *Hums as he gets settled at the workbench and begins his work, gently shaping and moulding the lump of clay that is Pot, who remains motionless, eyes closed. He stops and sits back to look at the clay from angles, then leans forward to do some shaping at one side in region of Pot actor's ear, miming giving it a big squeeze.*

Pot   *(Winces)* Ouch!

P.A.	(*Potters's Assistant jumps violently, and holds heart.*) Uhh?
	He looks around - there's no more sound. He looks relieved, fans his face and continues miming again pinching the clay.
Pot	(*Again, suddenly*) Hey, look out! Watch what you're doing! That hurt.
P.A.	(*Jumps violently again*) Huh? Wh ... wh ... what?
Pot	Can't you hear me? I said. Watch what you're doing!
P.A.	Uh, uh. Where are you?... Who are you?... W ... w ... What are you?
Pot	I'm a pot, stupid, at least, if you'll stop messing me about and get on with your job properly then I will be.
P.A.	But, I don't understand!
Pot	Oh this is really great, this is all I need, a thick potter!
P.A.	But pots can't talk ... well not at this stage in development anyway.
Pot	Wanna bet?
P.A.	No, I don't bet, I ... look, this is ridiculous. I'm talking to a lump of clay ... but I can't be, because half-made pots don't talk ... so I must be talking to myself. Which means, I must be going ... potty! Aarrrgggh!
Pot	I agree! But anyway, that's enough about your problems, now let's get back to mine! You've been messing me about and I'm fed up with it. You're squeezing me into a shape I didn't want to be. I never asked to be this shape - and it hurts too.
P.A.	(*Rallying a bit*) What sort of shape do you want to be then?
Pot	Well, I had in mind something taller and a bit more curvy ... with nice big handles ... oh yes and deep midnight blue, with a few gold stars. I want to be really trendy and go to a posh home.

P.A.	Well, I'm sorry, but you can't.
Pot	*(Abruptly)* What!
P.A.	*(Firmly)* I'm really sorry, but I said, 'You can't'.
Pot	You what!
P.A.	Well you see you're not actually being made into that sort of pot - I'm just an assistant around here, but only this morning I was given a very up-to-date copy of the minutely detailed instructions for the shaping of your good self *(Waves clipboard)* and they didn't say anything about tall curves or gold ornamentation. It's more than my job's worth to go and change the Potter's specifications for you, and ...
Pot	Hey, wait a minute! Can we just back up a bit here? What did you mean, not that sort of a pot? What other sorts of pots are there, for goodness sake?
P.A.	Well now, there's flower pots - beautifully lined up in rows in the greenhouse,
Pot	*(Gasps in horror)*
P.A.	Then there's chamber pots - tucked under the bed at night, and great for holding large quantities of ...
Pot	*(Cry of anguish)*
P.A.	Well never mind about them. No, what the Potter's making you into is a teapot - and my good friend, that's where I come in 'cos I'm on the spout-prep duty this morning, which is why I was squeezing your side just now ... that's where the spout's going.
Pot	*(Crying)* You can't, I won't allow it. Th ... there must be some mistake ... it can't possibly be.
P.A.	Well now, let me just take a quick rain-check here *(He flourishes the clipboard, takes pen from behind ear and runs down the list with it.)* ... yup, here we are 'workbench

	sixteen - lump of clay - becoming squat commemorative teapot named "Pot", for removal of lumpy blobs and application of chunky spout on Monday morning ... Nothing about being tall dark and handsome and absolutely nothing at all about big handles, I'm afraid'.
Pot	*(Wailing very loudly)* Aarrggh!
P.A.	*(Potter's assistant sticks fingers in ears. Speaking with difficulty over the sobs.)* Try and focus on the commemorative side of things if you would. You'll be one of the potter's new third millennial issue - limited edition ...
Pot	*(Continues)* Aarrggh! ... Aarrggh! ... Aargh! ... *(Pot recovers, coughing and spluttering a bit and pulling himself upright, sniffs)* but ap ... ap ... application of spout! I don't wanna chunky great spout sprouting out of the side of my head ... and lumpy blobs ... what a cheek - these are my beauty spots, my best features yet! Wait up though, I know what I'm going to do. I'm going to take this all the way to the top ... I'm going to call upon the highest authority there is ... I'm going to take this Potter before the European Court of Pottery Rights. *(Beginning to sound very self-confident)* Yes, this is all clearly a contravention of 'my rights as a piece of Earthenware' to be self-determining and independent. It's an infringement of my right to be an individual and to exercise my freedom of choice. It deprives me of my dignity and self-respect ... and ... and ... *(Suddenly realising what else has been said)* commemorative pottery, did you say?
P.A.	*(Nods)* Yes.
Pot	Commemorating the Millennium, did you say?
P.A.	*(Nods exasperatedly)* Yes, yes, yes ... Yes!

Pot	Umm, that puts a fresh lick of paint on the situation. I heard on Radio 5-Live this morning that this New Millennium we've just moved into is very special. It's ... it's ... well, it's a New Millennium ... er, it means 'let's look forward ... out with the old, in with the new' ... and it's all about ... time. Time for a huge dome at Greenwich - the glistening new 'O' on the meridian ... a time bristling with new opportunities and changes ... time for a fresh start ...
P.A.	*(Interrupts)* You should be a politician.
Pot	... and I'm going to start by taking my opportunity to change a few things around here, beginning with my right to have a say in how I'm shaped! Who can possibly know better than me what shape I need to be!

Potter appears from the back, moving slowly towards them. Potter's assistant bows reverently when he notices him approaching. Potter watches thoughtfully during next few lines, raising eyebrows/smiling gently.
Potter's assistant rolls eyes/makes neck-strangling gestures, etc, certain Pot's in big trouble, and makes apologetic gestures towards Potter.

Pot	*(Warming to his theme)* This generation is called, I do believe, the, 'If it feels good, do it/post-modern-third Millennium-generation', and with that thought in mind I say, 'Power to new-Millennium pottery, and every pot for himself' ... Ha Ha!
P.A.	You really know how to over-do a thing don't you Pot?
Pot	*(Glancing briefly at Potter but continuing obliviously ... clears throat importantly, adopts rhetorical voice, picking up on the politician idea with obvious relish)* Aha! yes, The New Millennium is about time, and ...

P.A.	*(Hisses)* ... it's about time you shut up I'd say. Pot don't you realise who's here ... the designer and maker of all pots ... including your outspoken and over-opinionated little self ... I have to say that for a squat little unbaked Pot you've got an extraordinary amount of bottle ... *(Aside)* apart from being a complete and utter nut-case.
Potter	Ahem *(Steps forward)*
Pot	*(Notices 'P' on his overall - sheepishly)* Uh oh.
Potter	*(Gently teasing)* My dear Pot. How good you look today. You think I have made you a little too pot-bellied h'm?
Pot	*(Squirms)* Erm ...
Potter	I think you are just right. I promise you weren't just some half-baked idea. I am pleased with your shape - a shape much sort after in some places I might add.
Pot	*(Still sheepish)* Oh *(Sniffing)* B ... but a teapot.
Potter	*(To enthusiastic nods from Potter's Assistant)* Yes, I've decided to create a tea set. Think about it you'll be useful. You'll never be alone and sad - you'll be part of a set. Some cups and saucers, a milk jug, and a teapot! You'll be full of warmth ...
P.A.	Instead of full of yourself ...
Potter	*(Frowns reprovingly at Assistant)* Trust me. You may only be made of clay but what I pour into you will be so important and helpful to many people. Then you will commemorate the real meaning of this new Millennium ... and the last.

Silence.

Potter	Trust me?
Pot	*(Softly)* Okay *(Smiles)*.

END

14

The decision is yours

Andrew Rice-Oxley

Characters

Nick Slickman *(Host/presenter of Bits & Pieces.)*

Jason Smiley *(Host of game show The Decision is Yours.)*

Shirley *(A contestant on The Decision is Yours show.)*

Raymond *(Shirley's partner.)*

Marcus Hail *(Questioner on Brainpower.)*

Lucinda Reigate *(Contestant on Brainpower.)*

Rev Jane Steadman

Father Tom Winhope

Bible background

Jesus challenges us.
'Who do you say I am?'
Mark 8.27-38

Scene: *A TV studio. The action takes place on the platform area of the TV shows 'Bits & Pieces', 'The Decision is Yours', and 'Brainpower', but the two latter shows are on the opposite side to 'Bits and pieces'.*

The studio audience are where the audience are watching this sketch. Pre-recorded applause on a tape is all that is necessary to represent them, plus occasional shouting out from members of the cast planted in the stage audience. However, the audience applause for Brainpower should be more sedate than the applause for the other two shows.

The sketch opens with Nick Slickman breezing onto the platform area to tumultuous, excessive applause. With smiles and appropriate gestures he tries to calm them down.

Nick   Thank you, thank you! Please ... you're too kind. Thank you, hey, hey, hey!   Really ... please, we must get the show under way ... thank you ... thank you! *(Eventually the applause subsides.)* Welcome! I'm Nick Slickman *(More applause)* and we've got a fabulous live show lined up for you tonight in 'Bits & Pieces' - the show which takes the bits you want to see again or missed the first time round and pieces them together for your extra special enjoyment. And tonight we have a super topic! A topical topic as you will see. Let me read you a postcard from one of our younger viewers - Stephen from Southend. *(Nick flourishes a postcard in his hand.)* Stephen writes, 'We keep hearing about the Millennium and all the celebrations planned but I've not seen or heard much about the man behind it all. I would like "Bits & Pieces" to see what it can do about this.' Well, thank you Stephen for the suggestion. 'Bits & Pieces' has done something and we've come up with some clips which prove the man you mention has not been forgotten. Certainly not! And in the studio to discuss the clips we have two Christian ministers - The Reverend Jane Steadman and Father Tom Winhope. *(Nick indicates the two ministers who are seated on one side of the platform.)* We invited two others onto the show but one said he didn't believe in chat shows and the other said he couldn't come because he was too busy getting ready for the Second Coming!*(Cries of oooh! from the studio audience.)* Well it takes all sorts, doesn't it? They don't know what they're missing, do they? And what are they missing? We shall see. First, a clip from 'The Decision is Yours'. How many of you remember this? Will she keep the money or will she go for broke? What would you have done?

He turns towards the area opposite the one where the Christian ministers are sitting and we see Jason Smiley, host of 'The Decision is Yours', with his arm round contestant Shirley, and holding a quiz card in his hand.

Jason Now then, Shirley. Do you want to go on, or do you want to take the £30,000 you've already won?

Shouts from the studio audience of 'go on' and 'go for it'. Shirley's partner Raymond, standing further away, is nodding madly. Shirley hesitates.

Remember, if you get the answer wrong you lose the £30,000, but if you get it right you treble your money and win a fabulous £90,000!

More excited noises from the studio audience and more nodding from Raymond.

Which do you want to do, Shirley, because, remember, Shirley - 'The decision is yours!' *(Pause.)*

Shirley I'll go on! *(Enormous cheers from the studio audience.)*

Jason You're a brave girl, Shirley. Are you sure? *(Shirley nods)* Well it's your decision, Shirley, and here is your question. Are you ready? *(Shirley nods)* This is a millennium question. Because it's about the man who started it all. Yes, JC Super Star. Now then, Shirley. A question about his life.

Nick *(Looking at his card)* Where, Shirley, was Jesus brought up? What was his home town or village in Palestine? Think carefully, Shirley, because if you get it right you win £90,000. If not ...

Shirley looks towards Raymond who is making signals at her, apparently tracing the letter B.

Where, Shirley, was Jesus brought up? He's called 'Jesus of ...'

Shirley   *(Blurting it out)* Bethlehem!

Jason   I'm sorry, Shirley. The answer is Nazareth. Bethlehem is where Jesus was born.

Appropriate reactions of horrified disappointment from Shirley and, even more, from Raymond.

Nick   And here's what happened a few moments later.

Shirley and Raymond are seen arguing bitterly.

Ray   How could you be so stupid? Everyone knows Jesus came from Nazareth - 'Jesus of Nazareth'. Nazareth!

Shirley   Then why were you making the shape of a B with your hands?

Ray   That wasn't a B. That was an N.

Shirley   A very roundy N.

Ray   You should have known the answer anyway.

Shirley   It was your fault for insisting I answered the questions.

Ray   Why didn't you stick with the £30,000? Why did you go on?

Shirley   I went on because you were egging me on.

Ray   I was not! The decision was yours.

Lights fade on Raymond and Shirley.

Nick   Oh dear, oh dear! Raymond and Shirley obviously had a few problems to sort out! I wonder if they're still arguing? Let's go over now to our two religious experts and see what they think of all that. *(Nick moves over and*

	sits in a chair near to Rev Jane Steadman and Father Tom Winhope.) Jane, can I start with you? What do you think of Shirley not knowing that Jesus came from Nazareth? Does that shock you?
Jane	I think if £90,000 was riding on the question I might have become confused too.
Nick	But, as Raymond said in the clip, surely everyone knows, or should know, that Jesus Christ is also Jesus of Nazareth. *(Turning to Father Tom.)* Father Tom?
Tom	Perhaps they should but they certainly don't. You see what you have to remember is ...
Nick	I'm going to interrupt you there. Because we now have another clip for you which may encourage you ... impress you even. Here is a clip from a recent 'Brainpower'. We pick it up where Lucinda is answering questions on her semi-final subject, 'The History of Christianity' AD 30 to AD 1000.

On the performance space where the scene from 'The Decision is Yours' took place we now see Marcus and Lucinda seated, facing each other.

Marcus	Which Pope sent Augustine to south east Britain in AD 597?
Lucinda	Pope Gregory the Great.
Marcus	Correct. On which day of the year 800 was Charlemagne crowned as Holy Roman Emperor?
Lucinda	December 25th.
Marcus	Correct. Which apostle's tomb was allegedly discovered in 813 at Santiago de Compostela making it into an important place of pilgrimage in the Middle Ages?
Lucinda	St James.

19

Marcus	Correct. When did the final split occur between the Latin church ... *(The hooter goes)* ... I've started so I'll finish ... the final split occur between the Church in Rome in the West and the Church in Constantinople in the East.
Lucinda	AD 1054.
Marcus	Correct. *(Gong)* That is the end of your specialist round. You passed on two questions. The date of the Council of Nicaea was AD 325. And the name of Augustine of Hippo's mother whose prayers helped to convert him was Monica. And at the end of that round, Lucinda, you have scored 20 points! *(Applause from the Brainpower audience.)*

Lights fade there and come up on Nick Slickman again, who is seated with Rev Jane Steadman and Father Tom Winhope.

Nick	Before I ask our invited guests what they thought of that amazing display of knowledge, let me ask you both about the first Millennium. Who for you is the greatest man or woman of the first thousand years? Jane?
Jane	There are so many great characters - only a few of them mentioned in the quiz. Paul, I suppose must be the greatest. Who knew Christ better than him? But I must say I have a bit of a soft spot for Augustine and saints like Columba, because of his celtic spirituality which appeals to me.
Tom	There were so many great individuals because each one, in his or her own way was inspired by Christ. If we consider someone like ...
Nick	We'll put that one on hold, Father Tom, because right now we're going to take a break. When we come back - 'Should we all know as much about Christianity as

20

	Lucinda of "Brainpower?"' See you soon. *(Lights fade and come up again to audience applause.)*
Nick	Welcome back. Well? Should we all know as much Christian history as that contestant in 'Brainpower'? Should it all be common knowledge?
Jane	Knowledge is good and useful but we must have faith too.
Tom	It's personal knowledge of Jesus Christ which counts. And he can be known as a person now.
Jane	I agree. It was that personal knowledge of Jesus Christ which inspired his first followers and all those great Christians of the last 2,000 years.
Tom	We must also remember something very important, it was the Church that ...
Nick	We're going to have to move on I'm afraid Father Tom to our next clip. Something a little more lighthearted at this point. *(Nick turns towards the camera.)*
Tom	*(Angrily)* No! You invited me onto the show, you've hardly let me say a word and you're now going on to something more lighthearted?! This 'bits and pieces' business just won't do!
Nick	I'm sorry, it's the show - and the show must move on.
Tom	*(Rising)* Why must the show move on? Where's it going to? We're dealing with something very important here - something we must all make a decision about.
Nick	*(Rising)* This is a show, Father Tom, a show!
Tom	True. In more senses than one. Let me read you something from the Bible. No, Jane will read it for us. *(Jane nods)* Thank you Jane. *(He hands her a copy of the Bible and she rises too.)*
Nick	I'm sorry there just isn't time -

21

Tom	This is a live show - we'll make time! *(Father Tom rises and approaches Nick.)* The passage is from Mark's Gospel, chapter 8.
Nick	I'm sorry, you can't do ... *(Father Tom puts his hand over Nick's mouth.)* Just listen, please! For a change!
Jane	*(Reading from the Bible)* Jesus and his disciples set out for the village of Caesarea Phillipi. On the way he asked his disciples, 'Who do men say I am?' They answered, 'Some say John the Baptist, others say Elijah, others, one of the prophets.' 'And you,' he asked, 'who do you say I am?' *(Tom releases Nick.)*
Tom.	He asks us all the same question today.
Jane	And the answer to that question makes all the difference.
Tom.	As it did to Peter and all Christ's followers since then.
Jane	Throughout 2,000 years of Christ-filled history.
Tom	So, who do you say he is? You, Nick. *(Points at Nick.)* And you *(Points at studio audience.)* And all you watching. *(Points towards supposed TV cameras.)* Your answer is vital ...
Jane	If you want to win ...
Tom.	Not a fortune - here today, gone tomorrow ...
Jane	But eternal life ...
Tom	The decision is yours.

Lights fade/curtain.

END

The train now standing

Dot Cameron

Characters

God

Iain

Joan

Jack

Bible background

A personal God who dwells with us.

'Lo, I am with you always.'

Matthew 28.20

The action takes place in the waiting room of a railway station.
Props: 3 travel bags, 1 book, 2 newspapers or magazines.
God is a voice off stage. Iain is sitting reading a book. Two other passengers are also sitting reading.

God	The train going to Plimsley, Plontin, Eardwhistle, Lee and Darth, has just left platform five, so if you're not on it, you've missed it. Sorry.
Iain	*(Looks up from the book he's reading)* What did you say?
God	The train to Plimsey, Plontin and a whole lot of other places has gone, so you've missed it.
Iain	I thought you were supposed to tell us when the train is due, not when it's left. Not good enough.
God	Hard luck. Were you going to Plimsey, thingy or what do you call it?
Iain	No, but that's not the point.

God	If you'd like to go to Tidson, Parston, Berry or Ickle, the train isn't coming yet. Sorry.
Iain	What are you on about now.
God	Delays.
Iain	I think you're having me on.
God	What gives you that idea?
Iain	For one thing, I've never heard of any of the places you've mentioned, and for another, your announcements are just plain silly.
God	I thought they were quite good actually. Amusing.
Iain	Look around. Can you see anyone laughing?
God	No.
Iain	Hang on a minute. It's you God, isn't it?
God	How did you guess?
Iain	It's just dawned on me that nobody else seems to have heard what you said.
God	I see. Why do you think that was, Iain?
Iain	Well, I expect they're not like me.
God	What's so different about you?
Iain	I'm a believer. I mean, I'm different.
God	*(Surprised)* Are you? You're not wearing a badge or anything.
Iain	I don't need to. Come on now, you know who I am. I go to church regularly, say my prayers, give money for good causes. I do lots of things.
God	What are you doing just now?
Iain	*(Exasperated)* Trying to read a good book, and if you don't mind, I'd like to get on with it.
God	You're reading my book?
Iain	No, I'm not.
God	What kind of book is it then?

Iain	A mystery story about a man who killed his brother.
God	There's a story like that in my book. Where are you going?
Iain	Seaside.
God	You're going on retreat. That's good.
Iain	I'm going on holiday.
God	Can I come?
Iain	No, I'm going on my own
God	Are you sure you can manage?
Iain	Of course I can.
God	So you don't need me?
Iain	No.
God	Might as well get on my way then.
Iain	Goodbye.
God	Bye then. Have a nice time.
Jack	*(Looks over top of paper at Iain.)* Big mistake.
Iain	*(Surprised)* Pardon?
Jack	I think you should have invited him along.
Iain	You heard everything that was said?
Jack	Course I did. You've made a big mistake.
Iain	*(Ashamed)* I didn't think anyone else could hear.
Joan	*(Puts away her book.)* We both heard. I'd change my mind if I were you.
Jack	You could be very lonely if you don't.
Iain	Why didn't you say anything before?
Joan	I knew right away who was talking and, to be honest, I didn't like your attitude.
Jack	Nor me. Thinking you're so different from everyone else.
Iain	Sorry, I didn't mean to hurt your feelings.
Joan	That's okay. We're going to Birmingham to see my sister, she hasn't been well.

25

Jack	We told God about it this morning.
Joan	He knew he was welcome to come along with us.
Iain	I'm going on holiday, though. It's different.
Jack	Why?
Iain	Because when you go on holiday you want a change from what you normally do. I mean, you want to have fun.
Jack	Don't you think God would like a bit of fun?
Joan	I feel sorry for you. You're going to feel lonely all on your own with no one to talk to.
Iain	You're making me feel uncomfortable.
Jack	What if you get into a spot of trouble? Who will you turn to for help?
Iain	Now you're making me feel worried.
Joan	You don't have to be.
Jack	Well, our train's due. Enjoy your holiday.
Joan	Have a nice time.
Iain	Thank you. Hope your sister's better. I'll say a prayer for her.
Joan	Changed your mind, have you?
Iain	What about?
Joan	Taking God on holiday.
Jack	If God isn't going to be with you, he won't hear your prayer.
Iain	I didn't think about that.
Jack	We'll be off then.
Joan	Goodbye.
Iain	Bye.

Exit Jack and Joan.

Iain	*(Looks thoughtful. Pause.)* Sorry, God ... God, are you there?

God	Of course I am.
Iain	*(Relieved)* I've changed my mind.
God	You want me to come with you?
Iain	Yes, please.
God	Not just because you think you might get into trouble on your own?
Iain	No. We'll have a great time together. Swimming, eating ice cream.
God	Can we go on the roller coaster?
Iain	Don't see why not. I seem to be quite good at ups and downs, don't I?
God	Never mind. Grab your bag, we'd better get a move on.
Iain	But the train hasn't arrived yet. Why do we have to rush?
God	We're on the wrong platform.
Iain	*(Surprised)* You were going to let me miss the train?
God	You did say you could manage on your own.
Iain	*(Amazed)* Well, I never did!
God	Come on, Iain. We're going on holiday!

END

Gods r US

Colin Lenton

Characters

Gareth

Mrs Little

Jesus

Bible background

Real God or Placebo?

'Behold, I stand at the door and knock.'

Revelation 3.14-22

Gareth dressed smartly like a sales rep. is led into a room by Mrs Little, the 'lady of the house'.

Mrs L. Do sit down Mr ... er ...

Gareth *(Extending a hand assertively)* Gareth, Gareth Smart, 'Deities r Us'.

Mrs L. *(Shaking hands somewhat hesitantly)* From the Spiritual Image Consultancy?

Gareth That's right. *(Holds up a briefcase)* I've come to give the no obligation demonstration. Thank you for responding to our advertisement. Can you tell me what attracted you to our product Mrs Little?

Mrs L. Well I'm sort of ... searching for something. I'm not unhappy as such. It's just ... you get to a time in your life when you look back and wonder what it's all been about and what it all means.

Gareth *(Interrupting)* And you need a bit of spiritual direction ...

Mrs L.	Er, yes, I'm searching for answers ...
Gareth	From someone wise and trustworthy who has your best interests at heart.
Mrs L.	And your ad said you were spiritual advisors ...
Gareth	We are indeed, and I'm sure we can help you, Mrs Little, for a very reasonable fee. But we can discuss that later. Let me tell you about Spiritual Image Consultants or SIC for short. We at SIC recognise that we live in the age of the supermarket.
Mrs L.	The supermarket?
Gareth	Think about your shopping, Mrs Little. We've never had such a wide choice. A few years ago we'd never even heard of a lychee, or sun-dried tomatoes, and your choice of shampoo was limited to greasy hair or dry. Nowadays we can choose a different shampoo for each day of the year! And we're not satisfied if all our shampoo does is clean our hair. No, it's got to be so stuffed full of protein and minerals you don't know whether to pour it on your head or your corn flakes! Choice is what counts. We demand it. And it doesn't end with groceries Mrs Little. Are you happy with your face and body?
Mrs L.	I beg your pardon!
Gareth	(*Hastily*) Of course you are! But if you weren't you could change them to suit you. Loads of people do it. Face-lifts nose jobs, tummy tucks, bottom lifts, liposuction, practically anything can be tightened, enlarged, reduced or in some cases moved to an entirely different location! Believe me, some of my friends have to take a tube of super glue everywhere in case something falls off! And with all the advances in genetic engineering, I bet you

designer babies are just around the corner. You'll be able to choose the sex, hair colour, may be even the IQ or personality of your child. And why shouldn't we? Change the world, even our children to suit ourselves. You never know, they might even invent an off switch for them.

Mrs L. *(Shocked and becoming a bit impatient.)* Yes, but I don't see what this has got to do with spiritual guidance.

Gareth Everything. Choice and convenience, Mrs Little. We at SIC understand your right to choose the meaning of life that is convenient to you. Which is why our product won't tie you to one particular view of God or mankind. To one philosophy or religion. With our product you can pick and choose the best bits from all of them, and chuck out anything that you're not comfortable with. *(He taps briefcase)* It's all in here for you Mrs Little. And it's all accessible from the comfort of your armchair.

Mrs L. *(Sceptical)* Sounds amazing.

Gareth *(Briskly, wanting to get on with the sales pitch.)* So let me introduce our company's finest product, the Virtual Deity Generator! *(Puts what looks like a pair of flashy pair of sunglasses on.)*

Mrs L. Well you do look pretty cool but I don't feel quite ready to worship you yet.

Gareth No, you misunderstand Mrs Little. This isn't an ordinary pair of sunglasses. This is a state of the art virtual reality headset. When you wear these and plug into the right software you will see an entirely artificial world created by a computer.

Mrs L. Gosh!

Gareth	Gosh indeed, Mrs Little! Using this miracle of modern technology you can experience whichever sort of God takes your fancy. And you can worship or pray to your chosen deity in any setting you select. Spiritual guidance at the touch of a button!
Mrs L.	But how?
Gareth	*(Interrupting)* The best way to understand the beauty of this system is to experience it, so pop your headset on, and I'll put mine on in a mo'. *(Mrs Little puts hers on somewhat apprehensively, Gareth gets out a lap-top.)* Now, have you experienced any sort of religious worship service at all?
Mrs L.	Well, I've been to church a few times.
Gareth	OK, that'll do. We'll select a traditional church setting then as you'll be more familiar with that. We can always try something else later. Right, all set? Now remember, when I switch on you will only see the images the computer generates. Your lounge will, as it were, disappear. It will appear just as if you were in a church building. Here we go! *(He switches on the virtual reality system.)* Impressive isn't it.
Mrs L.	It's amazing! So realistic! Wonderful architecture. And the stained glass windows ... so beautiful. Oh ... and those lovely flowers! Oh my, there's a man there! And look at all those people!
Gareth	Don't worry, remember he's not real. And neither are they. They're just the artificial congregation.
Mrs L.	They certainly look a bit artificial.
Gareth	Yeah, the graphics on the congregation are a bit rough around the edges I must admit. But you see, what we're aiming to create here is an authentic spiritual ambience

	without the hassle of actually having to go and join a church. With our system the church experience comes to you!
Mrs L.	Is it like a church service then? Are there hymns and a sermon and everything.
Gareth	Oh yes! The music group are over there, and we can programme them to perform everything from Wesley to The World Wide Message Tribe.
Mrs L.	Oh!
Gareth	And look at this chap! The virtual vicar! Programmed by the finest thinkers and philosophers in the world. You really are getting top quality with us, Mrs Little. You just place yourself in the virtual congregation, sit back, soak up the spiritual atmosphere of this fine old church, and your virtual vicar dispenses wisdom on any topic you choose from the comprehensive index. And all from the comfort of your own home! And if you get bored halfway through you can fast forward to the good bits. Or if you get caught short just as he's building to an almighty crescendo you can pause him till you get back. It's brilliant!
Mrs L.	Yes, but ...
Gareth	And for a modest premium you can get our delux package which even enables you to alter the vicar's appearance. Imagine Brad Pitt preaching in your living room Mrs Little.
Mrs L.	Good grief!
Gareth	Well maybe he's not your cup of tea, but you see what you'd have if you buy our SIC product. The building, the atmosphere, the music, the sermons ... everything that church is about, without the inconvenience and hassle of

	actually going and participating, no demands are made of you whatsoever. You are in control. Choice and convenience Mrs Little.
Mrs L.	Yes I see all that but is it true?
Gareth	Is what true?
Mrs L.	*(Pointing to vicar/speaker)* Him. This spiritual wisdom he's been programmed with. Is it going to reveal to me ... the truth about me, life, why we're here ...
Gareth	Oh, well, is there any such thing as absolute truth, love? Truth's a very slippery customer. We all alter the truth to suit ourselves don't we?
Mrs L.	But I want to know the truth that's real ...

Jesus gets up from the congregation and starts walking down to the 'stage'/acting area.

Jesus	And you shall. I will tell you the truth
Mrs L.	Look! That man's coming towards us. What's happening?
Gareth	*(Nervous, doesn't know what's going on, but trying to keep up appearances.)* Um, I'm not quite sure, this doesn't usually happen ...
Mrs L.	Are you part of the programme?
Jesus	Well Caroline, I'm here every week.
Mrs L.	How do you know my name?
Jesus	I am close to all those who are searching for the truth.
Gareth	*(Clearly worried now)* Don't worry. It's either a malfunction or someone's programmed in a practical joke.
Jesus	Don't be afraid, Gareth.
Gareth	I'm not afraid, You're just an image that someone's made up. You're not real. I can switch you off any time I like.

Jesus	Many people do, Gareth. They switch me off because I challenge them about the way they live their lives, because I speak into their hearts and say hard things. They think, 'Who are you to tell us how to live? We want to run our own lives'.
Mrs L.	But we must be free to choose, otherwise we'd be slaves.
Gareth	Good point!
Jesus	But you are free. I can't make you love me. You can choose how you will live. Now I stand at the door and knock, and you must choose. Am I truth or lie? Real or imagined? Choose.

Gareth pulls off his sunglasses, grabs his briefcase and runs out of the house.

Mrs L.	(*Hesitantly reaches out to Jesus and touches him*) You are real! Who are you?
Jesus	I am the way and the truth and the life. I have come so that you can live life to the full - as the Father intended. You won't be needing these any more. (*Removes her sunglasses.*)
Mrs L.	You are the Lord! (*Looks around, realises she is in the church that was in the virtual reality programme.*) But this is still the church that was in the programme!
Jesus	It is my body, Caroline. It is not bricks, windows, songs or sermons that give it life, but my presence in the people here. Now as you have reached out to me, and I have welcomed you, reach out to my church, and they also will welcome you with the same joy that I have. Remember I am always with you, even to the end of time.

END

34

The Ladder

Jessica Bryden

Characters

Angela

Anne

Fiona

John

Zacchaeus

Bible background

Is your hope in something that will last?
'grass withers ... but the word of God endures.'
Isaiah 40.3-8

A room. Characters are grouped around Angela.

Angela   I'd like to talk to you about this ladder. *(Points to empty space.)*

John   What?

Anne   Which ladder?

Fiona   *(Looking around)* I can't see a ladder.

Angela   Oh well, all right, not an actual ladder; more of a "virtual reality" ladder really. If you had that sort of ladder, what would you do with it?

Fiona   I'd use it to reach those cherries that grow right at the top of the tree in my garden that the birds get every year.

John   If I had a ladder I'd clean our upstairs windows myself instead of giving that lad five quid a fortnight to smear the bird muck all over the glass, like he does.

Angela	No, no forgive me. You're missing the point. In a sense you all, we all do, have a ladder.
John	What?
Fiona	Where?
Anne	My Alan's got three ladders - he's a window cleaner and (*Looking at John*) he always leaves the ones he does sparkling.
Fiona	I still can't see a ladder and I've got perfect vision.
Anne	Like crystal they are when my Alan's finished.
Angela	I'm not talking about a metal ladder you see, but one you can use to climb to somewhere in your life. Somewhere that matters to you.
Anne	People try to clean their own windows ... then they fall off the ladder and have to spend six weeks in hospital with a broken leg. You've got to know what you're doing to be able to handle a ladder, that's what my Alan says.
Angela	Perhaps I could talk to you first, John.
John	O.K. then, fire away.
Angela	If you had a ladder to climb, where would you put it?
John	That's easy. I'd stand my ladder against a wall where I could get lots and lots and lots of money. I don't care where it is. Could be in Timbuktu. Don't care what I have to do. I had nothing as a kid. Poorest of the poor, we were. I'm going to get some security for myself. And money spells security.
Angela	(*Interested*) Does it?
John	You bet it does! Big house, flash car, designer clothes, fancy restaurants, private education for the kids, brilliant holidays - but most of all, security. Peace of mind.
Angela	A good life-style then?
John	Got it in one.

Angela	And afterwards?
John	Afterwards?
Angela	After you've got the big house, flash car, designer clothes, fancy restaurants, all that stuff. What's next?
John	Next? Well, more of the same, I suppose ...
Angela	You mean like, *(Sings)* 'four BMW's, three Rolex watches, two Gucci track suits and a partridge in a pear tree?'
John	What!
Angela	I'm asking you what comes next? After you've had all that stuff. For years and years and years. And you get to seventy ... eighty ... ninety ... after you've had all that security and peace of mind?
John	You mean ... eventually?
Angela	Yeah. Eventually.
John	You mean when I ... er ...
Angela	Quite. When you ... er
John	Well, I'll have a big posh funeral, I know that.
Angela	Imported exotic flowers? Champagne truffles? Lobster Thermidor? Things floating in raspberry coulis?
John	Yeah, I reckon. And all my mates will be goggle-eyed when they see my will published in the Times ... when they know how much I've left behind.
Angela	How much you've left behind. Thank you for talking to me John. *(John exits.)* Now I'll come over and talk to you, Mrs Johnson - Anne - if I may.
Anne	Explain it again dear. Not a real ladder but something to help me along in life you mean?
Angela	That's right. If you had a ladder to climb on life's journey where would you put it? Where would you want it to take you?

Anne	(*Thinks hard*) H'm ... well ... I don't know quite where it would take me dear - but I do know I'd be going there with my family.
Angela	Fond of your family are you?
Anne	Of course I am. There's my Alan - told you about him, then there's Kerry and Emma and Tom. He's the baby though he's thirty-five now of course. Then there's the grandchildren - I've got ten you know. There's Joanna ...
Angela	(*Interrupting hastily*) You live for your family?
Anne	I've told you. They're all that matters. After Joanna there's Susie - she's ...
Angela	(*Interrupting again*) But what about ... afterwards?
Anne	What do you mean 'afterwards?'
Angela	Well ... one day you'll leave your family, won't you?
Anne	Me, never. I told you - I live for them - my family.
Angela	(*Gently*) I don't like to mention this but one day you're going to die, aren't you? You'll have to leave your family then, won't you? (*Teasing*) Unless you all go in the same plane crash of course.
Anne	(*Angry and distressed*) That's terrible! That's a terrible, terrible thing to say! I've never hurt you! I'm a good woman I am, anyone can tell you. I'd do anyone a good turn. You've no right to go upsetting me! I've told you about my ladder as best I can. I don't know where it's going do I? Nobody does. I just know I'm going there with my loved ones. Wait till my Alan hears what you said to me! Or my Kerry or Emma or Tom. They won't have you bullying me. Anyway I never go in an aeroplane - never have and never will. I don't want to talk to you any more. You've really upset me. (*Walks away from Angela as she speaks and exits*)

38

Angela	All right, all right, I'm sorry! I only wondered if you were interested in living forever, that's all. You and your family for that matter. But apparently not ... *(Spots Fiona, the woman priest.)* Wait a minute though, this ought to be different *(Raises voice)* Excuse me! Do you mind if I ask you the question Fiona.
Fiona	*(Brisk and efficient)* Of course not. If I can be of help.
Angela	Thank you. Forgive me, but I can't help noticing that you are one of that still comparatively rare breed - a woman priest. I wonder how that will affect your answer to the question, 'If you had a ladder to ascend on life's journey, where would you put it? Where would it be taking you ... in the end?'
Fiona	*(Sarcastically)* I am indeed, as you so adequately put it, a woman priest. One of the first to be ordained in the Church of England - on 23rd of April 1994. I'm sure you'd want me, as well as expect me, to be completely honest.
Angela	Naturally.
Fiona	I'm hoping, in fact, that I already have my ladder against the wall which will lead me to become the first woman bishop.
Angela	Really!
Fiona	Yes really. Why so surprised?
Angela	*(Momentarily confused)* I ... I'm just ... well, it's not quite the answer I expected. The first woman bishop, eh? That would make you some sort of career Christian, wouldn't it ...?
Fiona	*(Bridling)* That's not how I would put it!
Angela	No, I suppose not.

Fiona	Why shouldn't I be the first woman bishop? Remember Margaret Thatcher? Early on in her career she didn't have the confidence to aspire to be P.M. But she made it, didn't she? Why not the first woman Archbishop, for that matter? I have a double first from Cambridge. My administrative skills are second to none. I can pack out the cathedral with my sermons, when occasion demands. False modesty is just debasing God's gifts in us. As far as I'm concerned, career-wise, the sky's the limit!
Angela	*(Quietly)* I'd have said Heaven was as far as any one would want to go, really ...
Fiona	*(Angrily)* You're challenging me because I'm a woman who's ambitious in her chosen career! *(Fiona begins to exit.)*
Angela	No, not at all. I suppose I'm just curious, because your faith is apparently your career.
Fiona	*(As she exits.)* That's nonsense, of course!
Angela	I expect you're right. *(To audience nervously)* I don't think I'll ask her where Jesus comes into it, somehow. Well, I'm sorry about this. I've asked quite a few people and I don't seem to be getting the answers I'm supposed to at all. That's the trouble with these random surveys. You just never know who ... *(Interviewer is interrupted by Zacchaeus, who hurries in, carrying a set of steps)*
Zacch.	I'm sorry to bother you while you're talking to yourself but could you possibly tell me where I can find the new Millennium.
Angela	Pardon?
Zacch.	The Millennium. That people have been talking about. Where is it? What does it mean?
Angela	How long have you got?

40

Zacch.	What?
Angela	I said, "How long have your got?" It's just that it's a very long story. The Millennium isn't a place, it's a time, a date, a moment in history. It's the end of another thousand years, making Two thousand years altogether since Jesus was born.
Zacch.	Jesus? Two thousand years? Are you sure? Is that what it's about - Jesus' birthday? Two thousand years! I wasn't there when he was born of course ... but he couldn't have been more than thirty when I met him ... so young he looked sometimes.
Angela	You met him ... knew him?
Zacch.	Knew him? My friend Jesus, who forgave my sins and put my life right again? Course I know him! He was round my house having dinner a while back.
Angela	Sorry?
Zacch.	I said he came to dinner at my house a while back. Yeah, no wonder you look shocked lady. Everyone else did as well! The last person you'd think he'd take to, I was. Feathering your nest didn't come into it - mine was lined with mink! I don't reckon there was a soul left in Jericho I hadn't ripped off in one way or another! I don't know why I wanted to see him that much. Everyone was talking about him - maybe that was it. Anyway, it wasn't just my life-style that should have put him off, he was going to have a real problem seeing me for a start.
Angela	Why would that be?
Zacch.	*(Goes and stands next to Angela)* Use your eyes!
Angela	Ah, a touch vertically challenged are you?
Zacch.	*(Giving her a dirty look)* Are you taking the mick? Five foot nothing with your socks on is no joke when you're

trying to get a dekko at a super-hero. 'Specially with the place heaving like it was. I'd have stood no chance, I tell you, if I hadn't had me steps with me. *(Pats steps appreciatively and climbs them to demonstrate.)* but I got into this tree and next minute he's looking straight into me eyes and inviting himself to dinner! You could have knocked me down with a palm leaf.

Angela   Wait a minute! This is extraordinary! I've heard this story before. But it was ... You can't be ...?

Zacch.   Yeah, that's right - Zacchaeus. Short guy, tax-fiddler, fed Jesus, paid back money, got saved. Heard about me, did you? He's coming back, you know. To earth, I mean. Everyone knew it in my day. What if it's soon? What if it's now? Some time near this special birthday, this Millennium thing? Will people be ready, do you think? I was ready with me little ladder that day. God only knows why. Do you think he'll remember me if he comes now? Yeah, course he will. He's that sort of bloke. Fancy you asking me if I knew him! Course I know him! And all because I had me ladder in the right place at the right time to meet him - my friend, my Saviour - Jesus!

Angela   Everyone's friend. Everyone's Saviour, Zacchaeus. If we only get our ladders in the right place at the right time to meet him.

END

42

Platform Souls

Les Ellison

Characters

Nylon Anorak (A train spotter who never rides trains.)
Duffel Coat (Another train spotter, perhaps with a camera.)
Old Macintosh (A train spotter who remembers steam trains.)
Zipper fleece (A young travel enthusiast.)

Bible background

Are we on the right track or off the rails?
'Come, follow me.'
Mark 1.14-20

Nylon Anorak and Duffel Coat enter and stand as on a windswept station platform. Old Macintosh joins them. They search the distance to their left until Duffel Coat apparently spots an approaching train and draws this to the attention of the other two. The three spotters watch it approach, making the rhythmic noise of the wheels by slapping their thighs. They begin quietly, getting louder as they move their heads to watch the train flash past, and then fading away again as it disappears into the distance. They take pictures, check their watches, and make notes in their Spotter's Guides.

Anorak	You get that one?
Duffel C.	A Two-thousand ... an early one.
Old Mac.	It's just as well that they put numbers on 'em. This modern stuff looks all the same to me.
Anorak	I always said I'd give up when I couldn't tell the difference.
Old Mac.	If that's the case, I should have stopped long ago.
Duffel C.	Why don't you?

43

Old Mac. Habit I suppose. Anyway, someone's got to set an example to the youngsters.

Duffel C. Talking of which, I thought the young fella was joining us this morning.

Old Mac. So did I ... *(Checking his watch and looking out for him.)*

Anorak Running a bit behind time, is he?

Duffel C. Probably got sidetracked. You know what youngsters are like.

Anorak Yeah. Probably run into the buffers somewhere.

They are still having a laugh at his expense when Zipper Fleece enters. He is not quite the typical train spotter but has an obviously brand new Spotter's Guide.

Fleece Hi.

Duffel C. Hello there.

Old Mac. How do, young fella. Here, I've got your ticket.

Fleece Oh. We going somewhere?

Anorak Going somewhere. *(Laughs)* Dear, oh, dear ...

Old Mac. It's your special souvenir platform ticket, daft-head.

Fleece Thanks. Have I missed anything?

Anorak Only a Two-thousand, that's all.

Fleece Oh. Sorry. I've got the new book. See. *(Shows his new Spotter's Guide.)* It's got all the latest numbers. Some of them haven't even been made yet.

Old Mac. By heck. There's some stuff in here ...

Duffel C. Look out, here's another.

The three spotters watch and make the noise of the passing train as before. They make their records etc, as before. Zipper Fleece continues flipping through his new Spotter's Guide.

Duffel C. *(To Zipper Fleece)* Not marking it off in your book?

44

Fleece	All look the same to me.
Old Mac.	That's what I said.
Duffel C.	Only because you remember the Nineteen-hundreds.
Old Mac.	Oh, yes. The Nineteen hundreds ...
Anorak	Here we go.
Old Mac.	Now they had character, the Nineteen-hundreds. D'you know, there wasn't two Nineteen- hundreds the same ...
Anorak & Duffel C.	*(Mockingly predicting Old Macintosh's next words.)* Not like this modern stuff ...
Old Mac.	Not like this modern stuff.

Nylon Anorak and Duffel Coat laugh together.

Fleece	You don't see them any more though, do you?
Anorak	Well they only made a hundred.
Old Mac.	You know, I haven't see a Nineteen-hundred since ... well, since the Two-thousands come along.
Fleece	What happened to them?
Old Mac.	Don't rightly know. They just sort of ... disappeared.
Anorak	Two-thousands made them obsolete. Practically overnight.
Old Mac.	Now all that's left ... *(Sighs nostalgically)* is the numbers.

There is a pause as the Three Spotters remove their hats and stand as in an act of remembrance.

| Fleece | Book says the Two-thousands are the best ever. |
| Old Mac. | Listen, I saw practically all the Nineteen-hundreds and they just kept getting better. And more popular. Nineteen-hundreds carried more people than all the Seventeen-hundreds and Eighteen-hundreds and others put together. |

45

Fleece   Yes, and more people died in them too. Not much of a track record was it? If it was up to me I'd have scrapped the lot of them.

Old Mac.   Any more talk like that, and I'll have to ask you to leave the platform.

Anorak   He's only expressing an opinion.

Fleece   Well look at them. Look at the Nineteen-fourteen to eighteens. And the early thirties. And nearly all the forties. Complete disasters all of them.

Old Mac.   You can't go blaming the designer for the mistakes of the operators.

Duffel C.   And anyway the later ones were completely different.

Fleece   No they weren't. They were just bigger and less efficient. The eighties and nineties cost the earth to run.

Anorak   (*Looking down the track*) Look, if you don't shut up, you'll miss this one.

The three spotters repeat their passing train performance. They update their notes. Zipper Fleece makes no entry in his book.

Duffel C.   (*Noticing this*) Well go on. Mark it off then.

Old Mac.   You've got to get the numbers. It's what it's all about.

Fleece   I've got the numbers now. Look. A book full of them. (*Flips the pages*) I want to do more than just stand here ticking off numbers and marking time.

Nylon Anorak and Duffel Coat look at Zipper Fleece as though he is mad.

Fleece   Well I do.

Old Mac.   It's just a phase. All youngsters go through it but they soon come to their senses.

Fleece   I want to know where they come from. And why. I want to know where they're going.

46

Anorak	Oh, well. That's easy.
Fleece	What?
Anorak	Well, they don't really go anywhere. They all start off well enough. But eventually they run into trouble. Then they just come off the rails.
Fleece	Shouldn't we warn them or something?
Anorak	Oh, no. We only watch them go past.
Duffel C.	What actually happens to them is none of our business.
Fleece	But if the Two-thousand's don't get anywhere they'll just be ... a waste of time.
Duffel C.	We can't do anything about that.
Fleece	Yes you can. You can. Shout, wave, anything. Get noticed.
Anorak	Why do we want to get noticed?
Fleece	To save the Two-thousands. Get them onto a new track.
Old Mac.	Oh, no. The operators lay the tracks. They always have done. They won't listen to us.
Fleece	Then we make them listen. Look, there's protest groups. Action forums. Planning committees. We join them. We get involved!
Anorak	Involved?
Fleece	We tell the operators that the Two-thousands must have a new line, a new direction.
Duffel C.	We don't know anything about the Two-thousands. We've only seen a few.
Fleece	But the designer's seen them all. We talk to him. Find out where he wants the Two-thousands to take us.
Old Mac.	Take ... us?
Anorak	Dear, oh dear. Oh, no. That's not for us, no, no, no ...
Duffel C.	We prefer it here.
Old Mac.	On the platform.

47

Anorak	With a good view.
Fleece	For Heaven's sake! This is life. It's a journey, not a spectator sport.
Anorak	The Two-thousands haven't much of a history. They might be dangerous.
Fleece	Having the Nineteen-hundreds all over again might be even more dangerous. *(Makes to leave)* Someone's got to see the Two-thousands take us somewhere ... That's the designer's purpose.
Old Mac.	Alright then. If your mind's made up.
Fleece	I knew you wouldn't let me down.
Old Mac.	Aye, young fella. I'm with you all the way. *(Shakes Zipper Fleece's hand)* I'll give you a little wave as you go past.
Fleece	Thank's a lot! But maybe the Two-thousands are designed to go somewhere else altogether. *(Leaves.)*
Old Mac.	*(As if to himself)* Somewhere else altogether ...
Anorak	He'll be back.
Duffel C.	You think so?
Anorak	Nineteen-hundreds, Two-thousands. They all go the same way sooner or later.
Old Mac.	*(As if to himself)* Somewhere else altogether. I think I'd like to see that. *(Makes to leave.)*
Anorak	Where are you off?
Old Mac.	Buy a ticket. A real ticket. To go!
Anorak	What for? You know what happens.
Old Mac.	I know what's happened in the past. Maybe this time the future doesn't have to repeat itself. Enjoy the view. *(Leaves.)*
	Nylon Anorak and Duffel Coat look at each other, then at their souvenir platform tickets. They look up and down the bleak empty platform, tear their platform tickets in half and leave together. END

Sale of the Centuries

Edward Bennett

Characters

The Accountant

The Traveller

Bible background

Looking for real hope.

'there is one hope held out in God's call to you'

Ephesians 4.4

The accountant is sitting on a park bench eating his lunch. Enter the traveller.

Traveller May I join you?

Account. Yes, of course. Feel free.

Traveller *(Sitting)* I do.

Account. What?

Traveller Feel free.

Account. Oh.

Traveller Lovely day, isn't it?

Account. Yes. I often come here to eat my lunch ... if the weather's fine. Bit of fresh air, you know.

Traveller It's a very pleasant park.

Account. Garden of Eden.

Traveller We've come a long way since then.

Account. Eh?

Traveller Garden of Eden ... humanity has moved on.

Account.	I was speaking metaphorically. My little haven from the tedium of office life. Oh, I see my wife's put me two apples. Would you care for one?
Traveller	It's very kind of you, but, no thank you.
Account.	Aha, the Garden of Eden! They're quite nice really.
Traveller	Yes, I'm sure. You work near here?
Account.	Turn right out of the park gates, second road on the left. About five minutes walk. Makes a nice break.
Traveller	You have a busy life.
Account.	Could say that. I'm an accountant. Never short of work.
Traveller	Ah well, we all have to come face to face with the Accountant in the end.
Account.	So what do you do? No, don't tell me, let me guess. You're a professor of philosophy.
Traveller	No, sorry. I'm just a traveller.
Account.	A traveller. I wouldn't have guessed. So what do you travel in?
Traveller	Hope.
Account.	Eh?
Traveller	I travel in hope.
Account.	Ah, very good, very good. Don't you all? Big sales, boost the commission, bump up the bonus ... travelling in hope. Yes, I like it. But where are the cases?
Traveller	Cases?
Account.	Of samples. What you carry with you - to display.
Traveller	Display?
Account.	You know. You must show people something.
Traveller	I try to.
Account.	Well, where is it?
Traveller	(Patting his chest) Here.
Account.	Oh I see. All contained in a little book.

Traveller The book's important, of course, though it's not a little one, but what is most important is what's in here .

Account. Ah, that's it! Miniaturisation, eh? Microfilm? A floppy disc perhaps, slot it into a computer, tap a couple of keys and hey presto! All the required information at your finger-tips, so to speak. The modern way to travel. Get rid of all the baggage, eh?

Traveller Yes, that's the first thing, to get rid of all that weighs you down, and holds you back.

Account. I can see you're a man of vision; up-to-the-minute; always looking forward. No turning back for you - not even to the Garden of Eden ... metaphorically, of course.

Traveller That would be quite wrong.

Account. Eh?

Traveller There's no going back.

Account. Ah, yes, of course. In the world of business one is either on the way up, or on the way down. Never standing still. And I can see which way you're going.

Traveller Can you?

Account. Oh yes, always pressing on ... to the end.

Traveller The end?

Account. It comes to us all. Retirement; settle down with the stamp collection, or a bit of gentle gardening until - pouffe! it's all over - big black hearse; solemn undertaker's men; solemn music; solemn friends gathered round; solemn widow's weeds ... the end.

Traveller Oh no.

Account. Naturally we prefer not to think about it. Not much point really. After all, that's life.

Traveller Exactly. That's it.

Account. What?

51

Traveller	Life.
Account.	Life! Not much life then.
Traveller	That's where you're wrong, my friend. I told you I was a traveller ...
Account.	Yes, but you didn't say in what.
Traveller	Yes I did. I travel in hope.
Account.	Hope? What do you mean?
Traveller	I travel in hope that there is meaning to this life, a meaning that is gradually revealed as I seek it; that what you call the end is really a beginning, the gateway to a new journey, full of promise, with infinite possibilities, and alive with love and light.
Account.	You hope. Anybody can hope, but there's no substance in that. I hope that I shall win the lottery, but I doubt I shall be that lucky.
Traveller	Luck has nothing to do with it. My hope is not in blind chance, but in one who sacrificed himself for all humanity, and lives to show the way, who is the way, for each one of us.
Account.	Oh yes, who's that then?
Traveller	Jesus. Jesus Christ.
Account.	Oh, him ... of course. I wish you joy!
Traveller	Thank you my friend. And I wish you peace.
Account.	Not much of that where I'm going. *(Rising)* And I'd better be off. Nice to have met you.
Traveller	*(Rising)* You come here for peace. Your Garden of Eden you call it.
Account.	Well, you know.
Traveller	Yes, I know. But Adam was turned out of the garden to find his own way. He's still looking for it, but always there were signs to point him in the right direction, and

52

always he was shown a little more of what life is about. Then, one day there was a man who called him to follow. The way would not be easy, possibly dangerous, but the goal would be well worth the winning.

Account. What goal?

Traveller Not a garden, more like a beautiful city full of light and life and joy.

Account. You really believe that?

Traveller Yes. Do you?

Account. Me? I don't know. I don't know what I believe, or whether I believe anything. Will you be coming here again?

Traveller No. I must move on. But you will come, to your Eden, because this is where the journey starts. You know, we're all travellers really, and we must look out for the signs on the way ... and listen for the call to follow. Goodbye my friend. Peace and joy go with you.

Account. Goodbye.

Exit traveller.

Account. *(Watching him go)* ... stranger ... Friend?

END

A PLACE FOR THE DINOSAURS

Clifford Sharp

Characters

Uriel

Raphael

Bible background

God's Creation for a purpose.
'It is by faith that we understand that the universe was created by God's
word, so that what can be seen was made out of what cannot be seen.'
Hebrews 11 v.3

Uriel is sitting at a table with a roll of papers and a large clock. He picks up the clock and examines it. Enter Raphael who sits across the table from Uriel.

Uriel	At last. You are *(Looks at clock again)* 30 minutes late Raphael.
Raphael	Late ... what does that mean? Sorry Uriel ... you know I can't get used to this new-fangled time business. 20 past something or other. It's so confusing ... 20 past and quarter to. And these funny bits of metal *(Picks up clock)* that go round and round.
Uriel	They're called hands. *(Taking clock from Raphael)* I've been waiting while this one has moved from here *(Indicates 12)* to here *(Indicates 6.)* That's 30 minutes ...
Raphael	I thought they were tick tocks.
Uriel	That's seconds. 60 seconds make one minute. We've got to learn to understand time, Uriel. Otherwise we won't

	be able to work on the plans for this Universe that the Lord is making.
Raphael	Yes I know ... I'll try ... but it's so confusing. So where did we get to?
Uriel	We were trying to fit in the dinosaurs.
Raphael	I can't see the point of them myself.
Uriel	If you remember we began with the explosion ...
Raphael	That's what the thinking creatures will call the Big Bang isn't it?
Uriel	Yes, when they finally work it out.
Raphael	I'd like to be a tree if I had to live in the Universe. Reaching up into their sky. Much better than all the trouble of being a thinking creature. A tree only has to be a tree. I've just thought of a new type ... all its leaves will fall off and then after its been bare it will get beautiful fresh green ones. I'll show you ...
Uriel	Yes, later Raphael, later. We haven't got to trees yet.
Raphael	I like the cooling down time when all those volcanoes you've designed are still working.
Uriel	Yes, spectacular aren't they.
Raphael	But it does seem such a waste.
Uriel	Still worried about the dinosaurs?
Raphael	Them too. But I was thinking of all those lumps of fire .
Uriel	Stars.
Raphael	Thousands of millions of them in each bundle ...
Uriel	Galaxy.
Raphael	That's right. Thousands of millions of stars in each galaxy - and then thousands and millions of galaxies - but only one smallish star and this one tiny little ball ...
Uriel	Planet.

Raphael	Only one tiny little planet lost in all that space for the life forms.
Uriel	That is the way it has to be. ·I've got the equations here. (*Unrolls one of rolls of paper.*) It's quite simple really. If y equals the rate of expansion of the universe and x equals the force of gravity measured in ...
Raphael	(*Waving roll away*) You know I'm hopeless at mathematics Uriel. I even had difficulty with the simple stuff like relativity and quantum physics. Some of the thinking creatures will probably get to know nearly as much as I do.
Uriel	No they won't Raphael. Even the cleverest ones will be pretty limited ... stupid you could say. But we'd better start - we've got to fnd a place for those dinosaurs.
Raphael	I still don't know what the Lord sees in them. He wants them to be around for quite a few of your tick tocks too doesn't He?
Uriel	(*Consulting roll*) 163.6 million years.
Raphael	What does that look like on that ... clock?
Uriel	It means that this little piece of metal (*Indicates small hand on clock*) will go right round the clock 119,428 million times.
Raphael	And then the dinosaurs come to an end.
Uriel	Yes ... my volcanoes will start up again and stop them breeding.
Raphael	It does seem strange. All those different ones that Alatu has designed.
Uriel	You can't stop him. He was up to number 986 last time I spoke to him.
Raphael	And those long names that the thinking creatures will give them.

Uriel	Once they realise that they existed.
Raphael	And all those horrible teeth.
Uriel	You've been watching Jurassic Park - that's just the product of the nasty minds that some of the thinking creatures will have. We angels are only supposed to watch earthly films with beautiful thoughts you know.
Raphael	I get bored with the Wizard of Oz. I even begin to feel sorry for the wicked witch.
Uriel	The Lord will love his dinosaurs. They won't spend all their time eating one another you know. Not one of them will fall to the ground without our Father.
Raphael	And I don't understand this breeding. I've read the report on coming to an end ...
Uriel	It's called dying.
Raphael	Yes and I think I understand how it's part of our Lord's good purpose. But this breeding - producing new creatures themselves.
Uriel	Azazel is working on that but he hasn't finished his report yet. He's calling it sex. It should be ready for you to study by the time of our next meeting. It isn't just for the dinosaurs of course.
Raphael	I know. I've seen the thinking creatures with their tiny new life forms.
Uriel	Babies. But we're not supposed to go too far into their time.
Raphael	All this newness ... time instead of our eternity, life forms coming to an end, and then this ... sex. But I liked the ... babies ... I wish we could have baby creatures here.
Uriel	Well we can't. You'll grow to understand. All that the Lord makes is good.

Raphael	Blessed be His name. But there are mysteries about this Universe aren't there - things that aren't in the plans yet?
Uriel	Great mysteries known only to the Lord.
Raphael	We don't know how long the thinking creatures will be there do we ... whether they'll have as many tick tocks as the dinosaurs?
Uriel	You must learn to think of years - 31 million 536 thousand tick tocks equals one year.
Raphael	I'm only just beginning to understand tick tocks.
Uriel	Azazel told me that he thought that they might be able to decide themselves how long they stay on their planet. They'll find out how to destroy it themselves you know ... they won't need my volcanoes.
Raphael	Surely the Lord wouldn't let them ...
Uriel	It is a great mystery.
Raphael	You said that they'll be fairly stupid - yet they'll be able to destroy their planet.
Uriel	Foolish perhaps rather than stupid. Is it not very foolish to destroy your own home? And some of the cleverest thinking creatures will be the most foolish.
Raphael	How is that?
Uriel	They will say that their whole Universe just came about by accident - that nobody planned it or made it.
Raphael	Just came by accident!
Uriel	Just bubbled up out of nothingness.
Raphael	All the hard work we've done - that dreadful mathematics of yours *(Points at roll)* - all the trouble Azazel has taken inventing sex for them - and your volcanoes ...
Uriel	And my mountains and Esgar's oceans ...

Raphael	And those bluebell flowers that Isron was telling me about ...
Uriel	And apples for them to eat and the lovely blue skies ...
Raphael	And my trees ... my beautiful trees with their fresh green leaves. Just bubbling out of nothingness - that's all the thanks you get! Their clever people must be very foolish .
Uriel	Very foolish indeed.
Raphael	Perhaps they'll have a very short stay ... just ...
Uriel	Just a few thousand years. Their time on their little planet gone in a flash. Outlasted by the dinosaurs.
Raphael	By the unthinking dinosaurs.
Uriel	But you know the Lord ...
Raphael	He'll find something to love ...
Uriel	Even in the thinking creatures
Raphael	He might help them.
Uriel	But that is where we may not look ... a part of the mystery.
Raphael	How long they've got - whether the Lord will do anything to save them - all part of the plan ...
Uriel	Which even angels may not see.

END

A note about the authors

All of our authors are involved in drama in their local Churches where plays are tried and tested!

Edward Bennett *(Sale of the Centuries)* has at various times in his life been an actor, drama examiner, teacher, bus driver, headmaster, and run a theatre! He lives in Leicester and is now retired. (Except for the small matter of running a postal covers business ...)

Sophie Bishop *(The Good Traveller)* has been working for Careforce in her year out and is now studying Sociology and RE at Cardiff University. **Gary Kennedy** *(The Good Traveller)* is a full-time youth worker at Coton Church in Nuneaton.

Jessica Bryden *(The Ladder)* teaches English as a foreign language. She lives in Coventry where she is helping to develop a Christian drama group.

Dot Cameron *(The Train Now Standing)* was born in Scotland and is now retired and an elder at Hampton Park United Reformed Church in Hereford.

Les Ellison *(Platform Souls)* is a scientist and also acts as a local press officer for the Salvation Army. He has worked with theatre groups as far afield as Oman, and lives in Chorley.

Cara Grant *(It's About Time)* is a writer for Scripture Union's *Heaven to Earth* Bible-notes magazine. She works with dementia sufferers, has three children, and lives in Eltisley, Cambs.

Colin Lenton *(Gods r US)* is an occupational therapist and married with three young children. He has played the role of Judas Iscariot at Derby Playhouse, and attends St Peters Church, Littleover.

Andrew Rice-Oxley *(The Decision is Yours)* has been Head of Drama & Theatre Studies and an 'A' level examiner. He is currently completing an M.Ed in Theology and Religious Studies and an edition of the selected poems of Christina Rossetti. He lives in Crosby, Liverpool.

Clifford Sharp *(A Place for the Dinosaurs)* is a retired University teacher living in Leicester. He has been a prison visitor for many years and is currently President of Leicester Theological Society.

Reading from Nimbus Press

All our drama has been *Tried & Tested* before Church congregations or Christian audiences. We also publish Christian humour. If you would like our full list please write to Nimbus Press 18 Guilford Road Leicester LE2 2RB Or tel: 0116 270 6318 Email: sales@nimbuspress.demon.co.uk

MAKING WAVES: THE QUICK SKETCH COLLECTION
Stephen Deal

Author of the drama in *Hopes and Dreams* which has been on national tour. 15 biblical sketches which have all been performed by professional actors in front of large audiences - at *Easter People* etc. All with Stephen's hilarious and witty dialogue. ISBN 1 874424 22 5
"These sketches are unusual in that they are immensely user-friendly and *extremely funny*. A real gift to the Church."

Adrian Plass

EASTER PEOPLE: 9 SHORT EASTER DRAMAS
Les Ellison

Nine 5-10 minute Easter dramas for 2-3 actors. The angels, the caterers, the conspirators, the soldiers, the tourists, the lawyers, the gardeners, and the fishermen all by choice or chance becomes involved in the Easter story. ISBN 1 874424 52 7
Judged by *Stephen Deal* to be the winner of our National Christian Playwriting competition 1999.

ANGEL'S COUNSEL
Rosi MorganBarry

The biblical Nativity is cleverly and seamlessly woven into a fairytale about a King and a Queen. A wonderful treat for all ages. *Christian Play Competition Winner 1997.* (10parts, 30mins) ISBN 1 874424 86 1

THE PRICE OF OLIVES
Clifford Sharp

"I am delighted that this plays explores ... the Hidden years of the youth of Jesus. The Gospels show there were at least seven children in the Holy Family at Nazareth (Mark 6, Matthew 13) ... The joys and strains of family life are well depicted, in a community that was human as well as holy and serves as a model for our times."

Professor Geoffrey Parrinder

(5m 2f 40mins) ISBN 1 874424 46 2

SKETCHES FOR SEEKER SERVICES: 1

11 sketches originally used in worship and evangelistic services presenting the Christian faith in a way that non-Christians can understand. Christian approaches to crime and punishment, money, God and science, unemployment etc. and some modern parables. A book 2 is also available.
ISBN 1 874424 71 3

THE GOOD CHURCH GUIDE
Jonathan Curnow

At a meeting chaired by the mysterious Elisabeth, representatives of five churches in 'Lessingham' each argues that theirs is the true one that should be included in the new 'Good Church Guide'. Which will be chosen - the 'Bible-based' Free Evangelicals, St Stephens with its musical excellence, Blackmill United with its relevant social gospel, the Anglo-Catholics of St Botolphs, or the 'real' Catholics of the 'Immaculate Conception'?
(4m 3f 15mins) ISBN 1 874424 51 9

IT HAPPENED TO A CHRISTIAN ...
Edited by Clifford Sharp

A little book of Christian anecdotes illustrated throughout with humorous line drawings. True stories, some funny ... and some sad ones ... looking at the world through Christian eyes - preacher, child, teacher etc.
ISBN 1874424 32 2